CAREERS *in Your Community*™

WORKING
as a
PLUMBER
in YOUR COMMUNITY

Marcia Amidon Lusted

ROSEN PUBLISHING®

New York

Published in 2016 by The Rosen Publishing Group, Inc.

29 East 21st Street, New York, NY 10010

Library of Congress Cataloging-in-Publication Data

Lusted, Marcia Amidon, author.
Working as a plumber in your community/Marcia Amidon Lusted.—First edition.
     pages cm.—(Careers in your community)
Includes bibliographical references and index.
ISBN 978-1-4994-6119-0 (library bound)
1. Plumbing—Juvenile literature. 2. Plumbing—Vocational guidance—Juvenile literature. 3. Plumbers—Juvenile literature. I. Title.
TH6124.L87 2016
696.1023—dc23

                                        2014041087

Manufactured in the United States of America

Contents

Introduction

On October 29, 2012, Hurricane Sandy hit New York, New Jersey, Connecticut, and Pennsylvania. It was classified as a Category 2 storm, with winds, rain, and flooding that damaged and destroyed homes and businesses. More than one hundred people died, and even more were injured or left without power. Hurricane Sandy was the deadliest and most destructive storm of the 2012 season and the second-most costly storm in U.S. history, according to CNN.

After the storm subsided, many communities were filled with people who desperately needed home repairs. As the weather grew colder, they also needed help getting their plumbing and heating systems working again before winter set in. Among those who were ready to help, often volunteering their services or providing them at a reduced cost, were plumbers. Many skilled plumbers from the region and across the country offered their services on volunteer websites. In a household with a flooded basement, or one that spent days or even weeks without running water or heat, a plumber was a community superhero. These plumbers worked long hours, even around the clock, to help the communities in need. This was especially true in smaller towns, where skilled plumbers might have been in short supply and plumbers knew their neighbors well.

No matter where they are in the country, plumbers may have to respond to disasters on an emergency basis. Hurricanes and tornadoes can cause wind damage, and the storm surges and rain from hurricanes may cause flooding. Blizzards and extreme cold can cause frozen pipes or heating troubles. Fires and floods of any kind often damage homes. Extreme heat can cause plumbing and heating systems to

Many plumbers worked long hours to help homeowners whose homes were damaged by Hurricane Sandy.

malfunction. In times of disaster, plumbers play a vital role in helping communities get back to normal.

It used to be that the profession of plumbing was not held in high regard. Today, however, plumbers are respected professionals, appreciated for their skill and importance. It may not seem like it, but plumbing is one of the most important jobs in society and one that people cannot do without if they want to be healthy and safe. Almost everyone needs the help of a plumber at some point, and the work they do is vital to both homes and businesses. Some people are even beginning to consider plumbers in the same category as doctors or lawyers, in terms of contributions and sometimes even in terms of the salaries they can make. But most plumbers don't do their jobs in order to become rich. They do it because they want to use their hands and do a job well.

But just what does a plumber do, either as a community superhero in times of disaster or on a day-to-day basis? A plumber is an essential part of a community, whether the circumstances are dramatic or not. Plumbers do not just work in private homes, laying pipes and heating systems in new houses or fixing a plugged drain or a leaky faucet in an old house. It might involve the installation of a new septic system or the pipes that carry steam or gas from the street to a home or business. Plumbers are trained to do a wide range of tasks, both installing and preparing plumbing and often HVAC (which stands for heating, ventilation, and air-conditioning) systems, installing appliances like water heaters and fixtures like bathtubs and sinks, and fixing leaking pipes. Pipe fitters and steamfitters are specialized types of plumbers. Pipe fitters install the pipes that carry chemicals, acids, and gases, usually in manufacturing, commercial, or industrial settings. Steamfitters install the pipes that carry steam at high pressure, which is often used to generate heat and electricity in businesses.

Being a plumber, steamfitter, or pipe fitter also means that work can take place in a wide variety of settings, from the basements of homes, to the supply lines under a city street, to the complicated heating and plumbing systems inside a skyscraper or a large college campus. It is a job that can provide a variety of tasks so that no two days are the same, or it can be a job with a regular routine. It might involve being on call for emergencies at any time or having an unchanging schedule, depending on the setting and the tasks.

With such a variety of jobs and settings to choose from, what is an average day like for a plumber?

CHAPTER One

A Household Superhero

For many homeowners, there is no worse feeling than going down into the basement to find that the sump pump has broken and several inches of water are covering the floor. Or perhaps a leaky pipe in an upstairs bathroom has flooded the ceiling of the room below. Or maybe it's just time to update a kitchen, and the homeowner needs a plumber to install new water lines, a sink, and a dishwasher during the renovation. Whether it's a small repair, a huge emergency, or an exciting construction project, a good plumber is often the homeowner's own personal superhero.

A Day in the Life

What is a typical day like for plumbers? It depends on what kind of plumber they are and where they work. A plumber who does largely residential work may work for a larger company. He or she may start the day by driving to the plumbing company to get a truck and pick up the list of jobs assigned to him or her that day. A plumber who is self-employed might just need to head out to the truck parked in the driveway. Either way, the truck must be loaded with all of

Many plumbers work in residential settings, fixing things like leaky faucets or clogged drains.

the necessary equipment and supplies that will be necessary for the day's jobs. This might mean either gathering them from the office of the plumbing company or stopping at a plumbing supply store to purchase them. Then it's on the road to the first job.

A plumber who works for a municipality, for a construction company, or as a resident technician in a large school or business setting will just report for work at that particular place and either receive the day's instructions or follow a routine schedule of tasks. Plumbers who are doing installations in new construction will continue with a process that they began when construction started.

Plumbers often need to be available around the clock to deal with household emergencies.

Expect the Unexpected

Residential plumbers working in the community will likely find a variety of jobs on their list for the day. And it's never certain what they might encounter. Joseph Rosenblum, a plumber who was training in northwest Arkansas, talked about one experience he had with a skunk while he was crawling under a house. In an article on Marketplace.org, he said, "At least its tail wasn't facing me. I had a little bit of a chance to get out of there before I got sprayed." Rosenblum has also had to wade in sewage and make late-night emergency calls to fix broken pipes, but it's all part of being a plumber.

A plumber's day could start as early as 4:00 AM, and it can extend into late night if there is an emergency call. There are many different types of plumbers. One might be the man who is on call for a small plumbing company and has to go out on a call late at night to unclog an overflowing toilet. Another plumber is the owner of his own company and has to delegate the day's work to the other plumbers who work for him. Still another plumber might be a resident maintenance plumber for a facility like a college or a large office building. There are plumbers who design and install plumbing systems. A plumber may spend his or her day doing a variety of jobs, from replacing rusty pipes to unclogging drains that are filled with leaves or hair or many other things or installing a new dishwasher in a remodeled kitchen. Plumbing jobs are often a challenge, and they occur at all hours.

ALL IN A DAY'S WORK

Even plumbing jobs that appear to be simple can quickly become complicated. Matthew Sherman, a master plumber who writes a blog called *Ask the Plumber*, describes a job that at first seemed straightforward, doing some work on an old house that needed minor plumbing repairs. But he quickly found out that one problem only led to another:

> I slowly started to turn the water on, and this is when the fun began. Within seconds, a slow drip developed, right next to my head. The galvanized pipe was split on the seam on the top of the pipe. Water off, repair made- #1. When that was fixed, it was now time to try again. I slowly turned the water on, and a little bit further down the line, I see water pouring onto the floor. This time there was a crack in the threaded portion of the pipe. Water off, repair made- #2. This pattern continued for no less than 6 repairs before I eventually had to call it a day and plan on a round 2 the next day. By the time I was able to get the water on, 75% of the house had been replaced with new [water lines].

Starting Fresh

A commercial plumber has a different sort of day, although the skills needed are similar. A plumber who is helping to construct a new commercial building begins with the overall plan for the plumbing systems. The plan is first drawn as part of the building's blueprint, a document that shows where all the pipes, heating and cooling systems, and fixtures will go.

Generally, commercial buildings do not have basements like residential houses do. Instead, they sit on a concrete slab, or a flat pad of concrete that the rest of the building is constructed on. Some of the plumbing components, such as sewer pipes that connect to the city sewer system, are laid under this slab. These parts of the system have to be put in place before the slab is poured on top of them.

Once the slab is finished and hardens, more plumbing must be installed above it, in the lowest level of the building. Both below-slab and above-slab installations of plumbing can be tricky. The architect's blueprint for the building might not have the correct measurements, and the plumber has to make everything fit and work correctly inside the existing space. If the building has multiple stories, then as each new level is built, more plumbing must be set into place and connected to make all of the systems work together, from basement to roof. And while all this plumbing work is taking place, there may be other construction people, such as carpenters or electricians, also doing their work in the same space.

Before construction begins, during the planning stage, the commercial plumber has to make

Plumbers working on new construction have to coordinate with architects, contractors, electricians, carpenters, and other workers on the site.

a comprehensive list of the materials needed for the job. These include pipes, fittings (valves, vents, and faucets), and fixtures (such as sinks, toilets, and water tanks). Then the materials need to be purchased and stocked. Depending on the size and scope of the building project, the plumber may have approached different plumbing supply companies and asked for bids (written estimates of cost) for those materials, to find the most afford-able source to purchase them from.

Putting all the plumbing pieces together requires different skills, and a commercial plumber may be doing them all in a single day. He might be gluing together PVC piping for water. He might be solder-ing or welding copper or steel pipes. He may be testing the newly installed pipes for leaks. He might install all the toilets or sinks for a restroom and connect the water and sewer pipes for them. Or if his quality control checks show a leak or a dripping joint, he will have to stop and fix those problems before he continues on with installation.

Whether they work in residential or commercial settings, most plumbers especially enjoy the fact that for the most part, no two days are alike and there are always new opportunities and challenges that they need to work with and find solutions to. That chal-lenge, and the fact that a plumbing career can pay well, makes it a popular career choice.

Fitting Those Pipes

For pipe fitters and steamfitters, a day might be quite different from that of a regular plumber. These jobs involve installing and fitting pipes, valves, and

Some plumbers are also trained in HVAC systems, which allows them to work on heating and air-conditioning systems.

attachments; testing them; and maintaining them. Steam fitting in particular involves working with high pressures and temperatures in the pipe systems. Steam fitting requires a thorough knowledge of scientific principles. During the workday, a steamfitter might help move a huge boiler into a room at a factory or business. He may also have to read and interpret blueprints, drawings, and specifications for the systems; select pipes; weld, solder, and thread them; cut into walls or flooring to install the pipes; and then connect the system before testing it for leaks.

WHAT IS HVAC?

Some plumbing companies may also do HVAC work. HVAC is an acronym that stands for "heating, ventilation, and air-conditioning." HVAC technicians install, repair, and maintain heating and cooling systems in homes and businesses. Some may also handle refrigeration issues. There is a great deal of overlap between plumbers and HVAC technicians, and some people may do both, depending on the company they work for and the demand for these skills in their area. However, HVAC does require its own certification in addition to a plumber's license, so it takes more education and training to do both jobs.

Being a steamfitter or pipe fitter has an advantage for those who both like to travel and determine their own work schedule. Susan Miller, a pipe fitter who works on projects all over the country, including oil rigs, power plants, and solar fields, tells TheGrindsstone .com, "Sometimes the jobs only last a couple of

Steamfitters install, test, and maintain boilers and their pipes and valves.

months, and sometimes they last a year. You just work until you've built the unit and you're on to the next one.… I usually try to find jobs where I'm just working 9 months and go home in the summer."

Whether you're interested in a career as a residential plumber, a commercial plumber, or a pipe fitter or steamfitter, the job outlook for these positions is very good. According to the U.S. Bureau of Labor Statistics, these jobs are expected to grow by 21 percent by 2022, faster than the outlook for all occupations. This means that good plumbers and fitters will be in high demand. So how can you get started on a career in plumbing?

CHAPTER Two

You Can Get There from Here

As it is with many jobs, working as a plumber means that you need to have a combination of skills and training. Both of these are important because it will be impossible to do the job without both an aptitude for certain types of tasks and the knowledge about how to do these tasks correctly.

Knowing and Doing

The skills and abilities needed for working as a plumber are varied, according to O*net Online's Summary Report for Plumbers. First, the physical skills: Plumbers must have good manual dexterity, steady hands and arms, good vision, and finger and body flexibility, as plumbing can be a physically demanding job. "Thinking" skills are also important. These include deductive reasoning (applying general

Being a successful plumber requires both good physical skills for manual work and analytical skills for problem solving.

knowledge to solve a problem in a way that makes sense); inductive reasoning (being able to combine pieces of information that seem unrelated and form a conclusion); and oral comprehension (being able to understand what it being said, such as a customer explaining a problem). The ability to troubleshoot problems, make repairs, and actively learn new information is also critical.

In addition to possessing basic skills and abilities, the bigger piece of learning to be a plumber comes through training and knowledge. Not only do plumbers need mechanical knowledge about how building design, systems, and construction work, but they also need a basic knowledge of engineering

WHAT IS CODE?

Exploring a construction trade often means running into references to the building code. Building codes are a set of rules and regulations that have to do with the design, construction, alteration (remodeling), and maintenance of any structures in that city or state. They usually give minimum requirements for various building practices, to make sure that the health, safety, and welfare of people living or working inside that building are always protected. Instead of having to create their own codes, many towns, cities, and states base their codes on the model codes created by the International Code Council (ICC).

and technology, mathematics, and even customer service. These are the parts of the job that must be learned through training, either in a classroom or actively on the job.

Master and Apprentice

The plumbing trade uses the apprenticeship system. Unlike jobs where a new employee simply starts working and learns the job requirements casually as he or she goes, learning to be a plumber is much more of a formal training process. A person learning the trade of plumbing has to progress through a series of specific training and education steps. This ensures that he will learn and be tested on the knowledge he has to do the job correctly. It also reassures future customers that the person fixing their pipes or plumbing their brand-new house knows what he is doing, from the tasks themselves to the wider responsibilities of following building codes and safety specifications.

A plumber in training begins as an apprentice. An apprenticeship program may be sponsored by a local union of plumbers and pipe fitters, a union affiliate, or an existing plumbing contractor company that trains its own new employees. Apprentices usually have to meet minimum qualifications before they can be enrolled in an apprenticeship program. These qualifications depend on the state in which they are training, but they usually include being at least eighteen years old and having a high school diploma.

An apprentice program can last from four to five years and combines paid on-the-job training with classroom training, which may or may not be paid

Apprentice plumbers work under the direct supervision of a journeyman or master plumber.

time. The on-the-job part of the training should total between 1,700 and 2,000 hours for every year of training. It must take place under the guidance of a journeyman or master level plumber. During an apprenticeship, new plumbers learn plumbing codes in their area, as well as many different types of actual plumbing procedures. They learn how to install plumbing fixtures and pipes, as well as prepare and maintain water systems. Some apprentice plumbers also learn more specialized skills, like how to choose plumbing materials and fittings, identify different types and grades of pipes, and use the tools that are part of the plumbing trade.

Once an apprentice has completed his apprenticeship period, he will usually take an exam in order to become licensed to work on his own. However, training doesn't stop once the apprentice passes an exam and becomes licensed. He will go on to be journeyman plumber and eventually a master plumber. These require additional training and certification. Even though a journeyman plumber is licensed to work on his own, if he intends to move on to being a master plumber, he must continue classroom training as well as on-the-job work. Then he can train and take an exam to become a master plumber, who usually runs his own plumbing business or does more complicated plumbing design work. He might be employed by a larger construction company, by the government, or on a project-by-project basis.

The classroom training necessary for becoming licensed as a plumber at any level can take place in a vocational training school. Some apprentice and journeyman plumbers may attend a community or two-year college program in plumbing,

The classroom training for apprentice plumbers can take place at a community college or vo-tech school.

receiving a certificate or associate's degree. Some plumbers also choose to work toward certification in a specific area, which shows that they have done specialized training to gain those skills. For example, GreenPlumbers USA trains and certifies plumbers in water- and energy-efficient technologies.

Vocational Training

If students are interested in a plumbing career, what can they do to get started while they are still in high school and may not yet be old enough to work as an apprentice? Some high schools feature strong vocational-technical programs that allow students to start apprenticeships before they have even graduated. Many schools offer programs where students can begin learning trades like plumbing, both with classroom-type training and hands-on learning in a lab or even in a school-sponsored construction project. In some cases, schools have established partnerships with local

High school students may be able to begin their training as plumbers before they even graduate.

plumbers who allow students to work with them on real-life projects. And often the classroom training and hours spent learning skills can be applied toward the state requirements and count toward required hours and classroom time, once the student has graduated and enrolled in an apprenticeship program. This can shave some time off the apprenticeship program after graduation.

Many states are beginning to encourage students to not only start working on a trade in construction- and technology-related fields, where there are expected to be shortages of workers, but perhaps also encourage students to think about these careers when they might otherwise never have explored them. Vocational career training is becoming increasingly important in schools. An educational path that once was suggested to students perceived as not smart enough or motivated enough to go to college, vocational training is now considered to be the key to many occupational opportunities in the coming decades.

Students need increasingly complex technical skills to be able to perform in the workforce of the twenty-first century. The jobs of the future are going to need a deep supply of trained, skilled workers to do them. For this reason, vo-tech classes need to be just as challenging and intensive as any college-preparatory classes. Many students will actually use both college-prep skills and technical job-training skills in order to gain acceptance to college and then obtain a good job. And if they want a successful career, it's best to start planning during high school, not after.

What do students learn in high school vo-tech plumbing programs? A typical vocational-technical school plumbing program might include three years

FACT AND FICTION

There are many misconceptions about apprentice-ships in trades like plumbing and the kinds of students who decide to pursue them. According to the Montana Department of Labor and Industry:

Fiction: Apprenticeships are only for students who aren't "cut out" for college.

Fact: Apprenticeship requires knowledge as well as skill. Part of your apprenticeship includes the educational component, which requires you to take college-level courses.

Apprenticeship in the twenty-first century requires related instruction as well as on-the-job training. Many professions such as electronics tech-nicians, electricians, and computer repair technicians require extensive math skills. The dif-ference between a profession such as this and a more academic one is you immediately get to put academic theory into practice. Apprentices learn skills in the context of their occupations and the way that they will be used. Successful completion of a registered apprenticeship training program is comparable to a four-year degree relative to earn-ing potential, job security, and workplace portability.

of math, science, and plumbing theory. Seniors can work on a school's building project, where an actual residence is constructed, or they can go to work for a local plumbing company. In some cases, depending on the state where the school is located, a high school student can accumulate both work hours and classroom hours toward his or her journeyman's license in plumbing.

The topics covered by the plumbing curriculum in a tech school can include:

- *Water supply and distribution*
- *Sanitary waste and venting*
- *Gas supply and distribution*
- *Fixture and appliance installation*
- *OSHA ten-hour safety credentials*
- *Blueprint reading and estimating*
- *State plumbing and fuel gas code*
- *Applied plumbing mathematics, science and theory*

Students interested in a career in plumbing should check with their school guidance counselor or vo-tech department to see what programs are available to help them get started. Even schools without their own vo-tech programs are required to provide students with access to a regional vo-tech school.

I'll Be Watching You

Students who are intrigued with the idea of a career in the plumbing trade but are not ready to commit to a vo-tech or apprenticeship program might be able

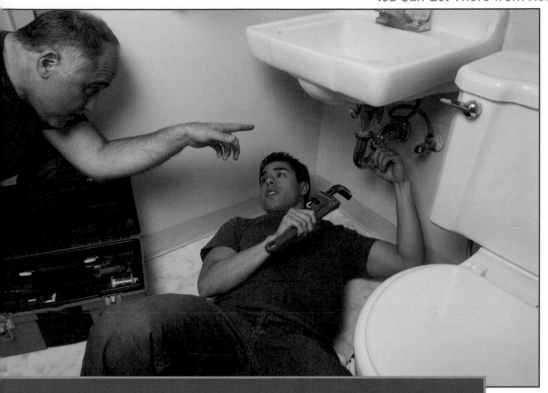

Job shadowing with a professional plumber is a great way to see what their job is really like.

to spend some time job shadowing. Over a day or several weeks, they can accompany working plumbers and see what their day is really like and the types of things they do as part of their work. Often it's not anything like what they think it is, especially if they have no previous familiarity with what plumbers actually do. It can be a good start to seeing if they want to pursue training as a plumber. Some high schools may have a job-shadowing program already in place, but if not, the school's guidance counselor or principal might be able to help students connect with a local plumbing contractor and set up a job-shadowing experience that way. Some community service groups may also have connections with local plumbers willing to encourage students who are interested in the trade. A community plumbing company, however, may require a student to sign a waiver of liability or follow strict safety rules while shadowing on the job, to protect both the student and the company against accidents.

So a student may graduate from high school with a solid ambition to become a plumber. It's time for professional training as an apprentice or in a college or technical training school setting. It's time to get started…but how?

CHAPTER Three

Apprenticeship

Let's say high school graduation is over, and caps and gowns are put away. For a student who wants to enter into the plumbing trade, it's time to enroll in a formal plumbing apprenticeship program.

Back to School

The first step to finding an apprenticeship program depends on the regulations of your state. You can start by contacting your state's department of labor or education. They will have information about training and apprenticeship programs, as well as any forms that need to be filled out for application to the apprenticeship programs they offer. In some states, a person who is interested in becoming a plumber's apprentice will go through the state to find a plumbing company to work with. These are usually companies who need workers and are willing to provide the four to five years of training necessary to educate an apprentice. In other states, the would-be apprentice applies for a job with a company and then enters the apprentice program.

Contacting your state's department of labor or education is a good place to start researching plumbing apprenticeship programs.

Often the sponsoring plumber has to sign a portion of the apprenticeship registration form. The form also asks basic questions, including whether the applicant has any felony convictions or has ever had his license to be a plumber revoked for disciplinary reasons.

Once an applicant has been accepted for the apprenticeship program, he must also determine where he can take his classroom training. Some states sponsor evening programs through their departments of education, specifically for training in plumbing and often at several locations spread across the state. Sometimes local unions will also provide their own classes, especially in larger

APPRENTICESHIP

The concept of apprenticeship in building trades such as plumbing has its roots in medieval-era Europe. At one time, being an apprentice in a trade was like being an indentured servant, where the apprentice lived in the master's home and depended on him for food and shelter in exchange for working without payment. Today it has evolved into an exchange of labor for training. In addition, modern apprentices are paid for their work and no longer live with their masters. It is especially important in building trades and other skilled occupations where there might be a shortage of qualified workers.

metropolitan areas. Technical schools and college programs may also be available for classroom training, and some states even have at-home, Internet-based training as well. Ideally, an apprenticeship program will offer classroom training close enough to home that apprentices won't have difficulty attending classes several evenings a week, after their regular work day.

Once a student has applied and been accepted into an apprenticeship program, he or she is ready to both start working out in the real world with experienced plumbers and learn the technical information that goes along with those real-world skills.

On the Job

The practical part of apprenticeship training means spending days with an experienced, licensed plumber and doing whatever he needs you to do. The apprentice goes on calls with the plumber and assists in whatever the job is that must be performed. It could be a repair, a new installation, or an emergency call.

What is it really like to work as an apprentice, alongside a working plumber? Not only is the apprentice learning a trade, but he or she is also developing an important working relationship as well. Apprentice Edgardo Morales's experience has been positive. He works with a plumber named Rick Hawley every other week when Morales is fulfilling the technical part of his school program. Hawley and Morales work together on plumbing tasks such as repairing pipes and sewer lines, installing boilers, changing out bad pumps for new ones, and any other task that a licensed plumber might do in the course of a day's work.

Morales says he learns new things every day and from "the best teacher I ever had in my life," according to shamass.org. "Rich is a great guy. We've worked on so many different things and I know a lot more about the business now than I did before." For his part, Hawley appreciates the traits Morales brings to the table:

"He's really come along. He's a great worker who shows up on time every day, and who shows enthusiasm for the work. He's very polite. He's mechanically inclined, that's for sure. And I never have to tell him to do anything twice," he added.

Repairing pipe valves is just one skill that apprentice plumbers learn.

As one apprenticeship informational site says, an apprenticeship is more than just classroom time:

Aside from the classroom courses that an apprentice plumber must attend, there is also the on-the-job training that you will receive. This is where the bulk of the learning happens when it comes to plumbing apprenticeships. It's about putting what you learn in the classroom into practice. Like other apprenticeships, you won't be stuck inside a classroom learning theories and doing classroom exercises. You'll be getting your hands wet doing actual plumbing jobs. You start with the basics first, naturally, such as cleaning tools. However, as you progress in your training and you learn more skills from the experienced people whom you work with during your on-the-job training you'll soon be assigned with complicated systems.

As valuable as on-the-job training is, though, the classroom component is just as important.

So Much to Learn

What kinds of classes does an apprentice plumber have to take before he or she can become a licensed journeyman, ready to work alone? The National Center for Construction Education and Research (NCCER) has a six-hundred-hour curriculum that apprentices follow over four years. Many states have adopted this curriculum in developing their own guidelines for apprentice training.

Members of the military can also choose to learn the plumbing trade as part of their training.

What exactly do apprentices learn in the classroom over so many hours? Here are a few of the classes that might be included in each year's curriculum, using the website of the New Hampshire Department of Education's Career Site for Plumbers as an example:

Year One
- *Introduction to the Plumbing Profession (5 hours)*
- *Plumbing Safety (20 hours)*
- *Introduction to Plumbing Math (7.5 hours)*
- *Plumbing Tools (7.5 hours)*

- *Blueprints and Plumbing Drawings (12.5 hours)*
- *Various Pipes and Fittings (45 hours)*

Year Two
- *Intermediate Math (10 hours)*
- *Reading Commercial Drawings (20 hours)*
- *Types of Valves (5 hours)*
- *Installing and Testing Water Supply Piping (20 hours)*
- *Installing Fixtures, Valves, and Faucets (15 hours)*
- *Introduction to Electricity (15 hours)*
- *Installing Water Heaters (5 hours)*
- *Fuel & Gas Piping/Fuel Gas Systems (30 hours)*

Year Three
- *Applied Math (10 hours)*
- *Water Pipe Sizing (17.5 hours)*
- *Potable Water Treatment (15 hours)*
- *Sewage and Sump Pumps (17.5)*
- *International Plumbing Code 2009 (30 hours)*

Year Four
- *Water Pressure Booster & Recirculation Systems (17.5 hours)*
- *Servicing Piping Systems, Fixtures & Appliances (20 hours)*
- *Private Water Supply Systems (10 hours)*
- *Hydronic and Solar Heating Systems (15 hours)*
- *Water Supply Treatment (15 hours)*
- *Swimming Pools and Hot Tubs (10 hours)*
- *Plumbing for Mobile Home Parks (10 hours)*
- *International Plumbing Code 2009 Review (30 hours)*

UNIONS

As with many other occupations and trades, plumbers have their own labor unions. Labor unions had their origin in the nineteenth century, when workers began banding together to fight for better wages

(continued on the next page)

Like many other trades, plumbers have their own labor unions for organization, for training, and as a collective voice to protect their interests.

(continued from the previous page)

and working conditions. Today, unions are still an organized group of workers, and the purpose of the union is to protect and further the interests of these workers. The United Association (UA), founded in 1889, is the union for plumbers, fitters, welders, and HVAC technicians. It is a national organization that has local branches throughout the country.

By the time an apprentice has finished this four-year curriculum, in addition to his on-the-job training, he will have learned all of the basic skills for being a plumber.

Will It Be on the Test?

After many, many hours of studying, training, and classroom time, an apprentice will be ready to take a licensing exam to certify him for independent work as a plumber. This does not mean that he will never have to have any more training. It is simply a milestone, meaning that he has achieved the first level of plumbing knowledge and experience and is capable of handling most regular plumbing situations on his own.

Plumbing exams are held by the state where the apprentice wants to be licensed to work. Many states now have online study guides for their licensing exams, as well as practice exams, and the best way to use this resource as an apprentice is to be studying the exam guide throughout the training period. This way it's possible for the apprentice to ask the experienced plumbers he works with about anything that he finds confusing, as well as making sure that he is learning what he needs to know for the exam.

This Certificate

THE CRAFT CERTIFICATE IN PLUMBING

is awarded to

TIM MICHAEL ORAM

WHO ATTENDED LOWESTOFT COLLEGE

Once an apprentice plumber has successfully passed the licensing exam, he or she is certified to work as a professional plumber.

In most states, an apprentice will submit an official record of hours worked and courses taken to the secretary of the state apprenticeship program or a similar state government department. He will receive a certificate of completion, which he submits to his state's plumbers licensing board. Then he will receive an application for the licensing exam, which is administered by computer at several sites around that state. Finally, if he passes the exam, he is officially a journeyman-level plumber.

What will be included on a plumbing license exam? That varies from state to state. Some states use questions based on the uniform plumbing code, as well as adding questions that might measure specific knowledge for that state's additions to the code. For example, a state such as California, where earthquakes are frequent, might have questions on its exam that have to do with special building codes developed for earthquake situations. The exam will also usually have several sections with both questions and practical exercise such as drawing diagrams or designing a piping system.

This example is from the plumbing exam for the state of Washington. The examination consists of three parts:

1. Technical and general trade knowledge. This part of the exam is one hundred questions on plumbing code.

2. Code application knowledge for waste and vents. This part of the exam is a waste and vent sizing exercise. You will be provided with a drawing of a building showing elevated views of plumbing fixtures along with the illustrated piping for the vents, waste, and cleanouts that are needed to drain and vent these fixtures. You will provide fixture units and pipe sizes. Use minimum sizing as allowed by the UPC along with maintaining aggregate venting.

3. Code application for water piping. This part of the exam is a water pipe sizing exercise. You will be provided with a drawing of a building showing elevated views of plumbing fixtures along with the illustrated piping for the hot and

cold water distribution system. You will provide the fixture units and pipe sizes. Use minimum sizing as allowed by the UPC.

This test includes both general knowledge questions and demonstrating an ability to take that knowledge and create systems or code applications for it. States vary as to what is included in their exams, but the basics are usually the same.

Hopefully, after four or five years of training and experience in an apprenticeship program, the apprentice will pass the exam with flying colors and become, officially, a journeyman plumber. It is an exciting milestone, but it is also a time to make some big decisions about what comes next.

CHAPTER Four

Now You're Plumbing!

Once an apprentice plumber has passed the licensing exam to become a journeyman plumber, there are several options to explore while performing the job. The simplest one is for the apprentice to continue working for the plumbing contractor or company that he or she apprenticed with. One advantage of this option is that the apprentice has already established a good working relationship with the contractor or company and won't have to begin all over again with a new one. A journeyman plumber who intends to work toward a master's license will also have the advantage of continuing to work with more experienced plumbers for additional on-the job training.

The other option is to go to work for a different company or perhaps even in a different type of setting, such as being a resident plumber at a college or institution or for a city building department. The advantage to this option is the chance to gain broader experience with a different company or a different setting. If the apprentice did not have a possitive experience during the apprenticeship, this might be a good option.

COMPUTER SKILLS

Anyone who is planning to work as a plumber should become familiar with computers and the software that makes plumbing work easier. All plumbers, pipe fitters, and steamfitters will have to read blueprints, follow specific instructions from the builders or contractors they might be working for, plan out work and plumbing systems, and generally do these things capably and efficiently. And since almost all of these things are now done using computers, both to plan and keep track of progress, a plumber really needs to have good computer skills. For example, if a plumber is installing the plumbing system in a brand-new residential home, a computer can help him or her create a specific, detailed plan that shows where every part of the plumbing system goes, from pipes to fixtures, and even what materials might be needed for the job.

Journeyman to Master

What exactly is involved in the journeyman stage of being a plumber? Journeyman plumbers are fully trained and licensed to perform any plumbing work, whether it is basic household plumbing or a more specialized field, if that is what they trained for during their apprenticeship. Once they have passed the journeyman's exam, they are considered to be skilled, experienced plumbers who have all the skills they

Training to become a plumber at any level means working under the guidance of more experienced plumbers.

need to perform their job well. However, while a journeyman is now certified as being able to perform all the jobs that an experienced plumber does, he or she does not usually manage projects or supervise other employees. This is usually the job of a master plumber, and journeyman plumbers will not make as much money as the master plumber does.

If a journeyman plumber is interested in starting his or her own plumbing business, then it will be necessary to pursue a master plumbing license. A master plumber is highly experienced and has advanced knowledge of areas such as installation, repair, and maintenance. In most states, a plumber can start a plumbing company and act as an employer or contractor only if he or she has a master plumber's license. Only master plumbers can supervise journeyman-level plumbers. In addition to being able to perform any type of plumbing work, a master plumber is also responsible for evaluating new job orders, coordinating the work for those orders and assigning it to employees, and meeting with customers or potential clients to review their needs and problems.

As with apprentices taking an exam to become journeyman plumbers, a journeyman plumber who wants to be licensed as a master plumber must have four to five years of experience at the journeyman level and then take a state exam for a master plumber license. After earning this certification, a master plumber can start his or her own company and employ apprentice and journeyman plumbers.

There are many advantages to pursuing the status of master plumber and being self-employed. Aside from the advanced knowledge gained and responsibilities undertaken, master plumbers earn higher salaries than journeyman plumbers. There is also the freedom of owning one's own company: many people would rather be their own boss than work for someone else. On the other hand, master plumbers who own their own companies must also deal with many administrative details, such as cash flow, hiring and firing, and accounting. This is a lot of work and can lead to many headaches. For this reason, some plumbers are content to remain at journeyman level and work for another company, rather than having the responsibility of running a business.

It's Your Business

If eventually owning your own plumbing business is your long-term goal, then it is helpful to know just what is involved in starting a plumbing company.

As stated, the most important part of starting a plumbing business is having state certification and licenses, which prove that you know your trade and that customers can trust you with their work. Then it is necessary to set up an office of some kind, which for an independent plumber working alone may simply be part of his or her home. As with any office, it will need to have a computer, phone, fax, and office equipment and furnishings.

It is necessary to have a vehicle, not only to travel to plumbing jobs, but also as a place to keep parts needed for the most common plumbing jobs and to carry equipment. Most plumbers use a van or larger commercial truck.

A plumber will need to prepare for the business of getting work. Advertising is important, and since many plumbers find work through word-of-mouth referrals

One of the basic necessities for a plumbing business is a vehicle for transportation to jobs and for storing parts and equipment.

from customers, it is also helpful to establish customer loyalty and referral programs where customers get discounts for referrals. Not only does a plumbing business need to be advertised online and locally in phone books and newspapers, but a plumber must also learn how to calculate and submit bids. For many plumbing jobs, especially installations for building contractors, the builder will ask several plumbing companies to submit a bid, or the dollar amount they can perform the job for. Ideally, the bid should be competitive but still pay the plumber's costs of doing business and make a small profit as well.

FRANCHISE

One other possibility for master plumbers who do not want full responsibility for the business aspects of a plumbing company is to buy into a plumbing franchise. A franchise is an established trademarked business. Individuals may pay a fee to the corporation and operate their own business using the corporation's name. Examples of existing plumbing franchises are Roto-Rooter and Mr. Rooter.

Buying an established plumbing franchise can be easier than running an independent plumbing business.

In order to run a franchise, individuals have to pay a fee to the corporation in order to be part of the franchise. They also need to purchase all the necessary tools and equipment. But running a franchise can be easier than starting a business from scratch because franchise owners benefit from many aspects of a larger corporation, including name recognition, marketing and advertising, established business practices, and corporate support. It can also be an advantage in poor economic times, since it may be cheaper for plumbers to run a franchise than to run their own business.

Other Places to Work

If starting a plumbing business isn't appealing, a journeyman or master plumber can explore job opportunities in areas other than residential repair and construction. Many industries need the skills of plumbers, such as shipbuilding, power plants, and the military.

Large shipbuilding companies that construct ships for commercial and military purposes need plumbers because the water fittings and water supply systems in a ship have to be perfect. Plumbers have the proper knowledge and skills about the mechanics of pipes and plumbing systems. Plumbers also create emergency plans for situations that could arise when ships are out at sea. Shipbuilding is an industry where journeyman plumbers can find employment without having to achieve a master's license.

Ships require trained plumbers to install and maintain water fittings, piping, and water supply systems.

Power plants, oil rigs, and solar power facilities also require plumbers to install pipe systems for water or steam. Many of these jobs are done by pipe fitters and steamfitters, who specialize in constructing systems that can handle high pressure and high temperatures. These professionals begin with basic plumbing training and then specialize as fitters, usually by apprenticing with someone in those industries. Pipe fitters are usually working with pressurized pipes. These pipes might have to withstand low pressure or high pressure, depending on what they are used for. These pressure systems are usually found in commercial buildings like hydroelectric power plants, factories, or large central air-conditioning or heating systems. Pipe fitters install these systems and then maintain and repair them when necessary. And since automatic controls are being used more and more often to run these systems, pipe fitters may have to install and maintain those as well.

Because fitters are often performing large-scale work on plants under construction, they can travel a great deal and often set their own schedules of time on the job and time at home. The downside is that they are subject to the changing state of the construction industry. During economic recessions, when there is not as much new construction, they may not have enough work, whereas residential plumbers usually have enough work no matter what the economy because homes will always need plumbing repairs.

The military is another place where plumbers can find work. Usually, those who enlist in the military receive their training as part of their military career. They must pass a vocational aptitude test to make sure that they have minimal skills and abilities for the plumbing specialization, but once they are enrolled in the program, they can receive the equivalent of apprenticeship training while actively enlisted in the military. When their term of enlistment is over, they can either continue to work in the military as a plumber or use their apprenticeship credentials to take the civilian licensing exam and start a civilian plumbing career.

Even in combat situations, military plumbers are vital for repairing water purification and supply systems.

Plumber training in the army is similar to a civilian apprentice program but with some different elements that relate to the possibility of deployment overseas or in combat-based situations. Army plumbers have to take the same ten weeks of basic training that all new army recruits take, but then they complete another seven weeks of advanced individual training, where they learn about plumbing. The training includes time in the classroom as well as on-the-job instruction and experience, including learning to use carpentry and masonry tools. Some of the skills that army plumbers learn include installing and repairing pipes, plumbing fixtures, and systems for purifying and distilling water, which are especially important in foreign locations. They might also learn to maintain and repair hydraulic (water) and pneumatic (air) systems.

Basically, once an apprentice plumber earns journeyman or even master plumber status, there are many possibilities for employment, from local plumbing contractors all the way to global travel opportunities in industrial construction. It all depends on a new plumber's career goals. No matter where they work, however, plumbers are valuable assets to their communities and organizations as a result of the services they provide.

CHAPTER Five

The Future's So Bright

It's no secret that a trained, reliable, established plumber is an extremely valuable asset to any community, no matter how large or small. But plumbers are actually much more important to the world, so much so that there is a World Plumbing Day on March 11 of every year. Many historians even believe that plumbing is the number one invention in history because it helped control disease and made human life healthier and more sanitary. Even today the health of the people of the world depends on plumbers for clean drinking water and effective sanitation systems. According to the World Plumbing Day website:

> The statistics are sobering. According to the World Health Organization 1.1 billion people do not have access to safe clean water supplies and 2.6 billion do not enjoy the use of effective sanitation systems. The tragic result is 3.1 million children die each year as a result of diseases that could have been prevented if only the children had access to basic facilities. World Plumbing Day raises awareness and

salutes the integral role plumbers play to not only protect citizens' health and safety—but to boldly pursue innovations that improve lives.

The United Nations declared 2005–2015 the International Decade for Action "Water for Life," setting a world agenda that focuses increased attention on water-related issues. The goal was to increase access to clean water and good sanitation, all over the world.

HUG A PLUMBER

In addition to World Plumbing Day, there is also National Plumber's Day in the United States, observed every April 25. Also called "Hug a Plumber" Day, it is a day set aside to thank plumbers for the important services they provide to their communities. According to directenergy.com, "Consider what your morning routine would have been like today, without safe, clean, water; indoor plumbing; and the kitchen sink. We often take these conveniences for granted until we are stuck and need a plumber. New innovations in plumbing have taken us from the time of Benjamin Franklin and water closets to new water saving gadgets in our kitchens and bathrooms and instant hot water. Every day, plumbers work to keep our water running, drains and pipes flowing and to solve plumbing related issues. They also offer solutions to help improve water quality, water savings and water flow in and around your home. That certainly deserves a hug."

Plumbers Are "Bright"

In addition to the importance of the plumbing profession to the overall health of the world, it is also increasingly important at home. Climate change and the increasing incidents of natural disasters such as hurricanes and flooding mean that plumbers will be needed for emergency preparations and repairs. New building codes and green technologies also require experts in the plumbing field. According to the U.S. Bureau of Labor Statistics, jobs for plumbers, pipe fitters, and steamfitters are projected to grow faster than the average for all other occupations, at a rate of about 21 percent between 2012 and 2022. This is because the demand for plumbers and fitters is going to grow based on the amount of new construction and the need for more water-efficient plumbing systems. And as new power plants and factories are constructed, more steamfitters and pipe fitters will be needed to help build them. There are also some states that have adopted changes to the International Residential Code for building, which requires all new single- and double-family homes to have sprinkler systems installed. Putting these systems in place requires plumbers.

And although the demand is increasing, many current plumbers will be retiring over the next ten years, and there is already a shortage of qualified plumbers to replace them. For this reason, the occupation of plumbers, pipe fitters, and steamfitters is classified as "bright," which means that these occupations "are expected to grow rapidly [much faster than the average] in the next several years, will have large numbers of job openings [100,000 or more new jobs in the next ten years], or are new and emerging occupations."

New building codes and technologies will require an increasing number of trained plumbers.

It's a Greener World

The new and emerging jobs in the plumbing trade have to do with the growing movement toward "green" technologies. Green building, which is also known as green construction or sustainable building, requires using green processes and materials to construct buildings, as well as systems that make them more energy-efficient and environmentally friendly to operate. Green buildings use resources efficiently, protect the health and safety of inhabitants, and reduce pollution and waste. According to the U.S. Environmental Protection Agency, green building means "increasing the efficiency with which buildings and their sites use and harvest energy, water, and materials; and protecting and restoring human health and the environment, throughout the building life-cycle: siting, design, construction, operation, maintenance, renovation and deconstruction."

According to O*net Online, the tasks that plumbers are increasingly performing for the green construction industry include:

- *Calculating costs or savings for water- or energy-efficient appliances or systems*
- *Compiling information on governmental incentive programs related to the installation of energy- or water-saving plumbing systems or devices*
- *Determining sizing requirements for solar hot-water heating systems, taking into account factors such as site orientation, load calculations, or storage capacity requirements*

Climate change and increasingly severe natural disasters mean that more plumbers will be needed to cope with damage to homes and businesses.

- *Installing alternative water sources, such as rainwater harvesting systems or graywater reuse systems*
- *Installing green plumbing equipment, such as faucet flow restrictors, dual-flush or pressure-assisted flush toilets, or tankless hot-water heaters*
- *Installing, testing, or commissioning solar thermal or solar photovoltaic hot-water heating systems*
- *Performing domestic plumbing audits to identify ways in which customers might reduce consumption of water or energy*

New green plumbing technologies include dual flush toilets that conserve water.

• Recommending energy- or water-saving products, such as low-flow faucets or shower heads, water-saving toilets, or high-efficiency hot-water heaters

• Welding small pipes or special piping using specialized techniques, equipment, or materials, such as computer-assisted welding or microchip fabrication

As the world begins to experience the effects of climate change, as well as the need to find cheaper and renewable sources of energy, plumbers are becoming even more vital in helping translate new technologies, such as solar power and reducing the consumption of water and fossil fuels, into regular homes across the country. And as green buildings and resource conservation become more common, there will be a need for more plumbers in every local community who can work with these technologies and help people make their homes more green and efficient.

WHERE ARE PLUMBERS WORKING?

The U.S. Bureau of Labor Statistics has a chart that shows the industries where plumbers are employed and how many work in each industry. Some of the surprising places where plumbers and fitters work include mining, quarrying, and oil and gas extraction and pipelines. Plumbers also work in manufacturing—things like paper, petroleum, resins, iron and steel, pharmaceuticals, and machinery. They may work on railroad or other transportation services. Some work in scientific research or education or in engineering or architectural services. There are few limits on the areas where a licensed plumber can be employed. You can find the specifics at http://www.bls.gov/emp/ind-occ-matrix/occ_xls/occ_47-2152.xls

A Community of Plumbers

As the number of plumbers increases, new and established members of the plumbing trade can rely on professional organizations to help them stay current with technology and building codes and other vital information. Labor unions, like the United Association (UA) for plumbers and fitters, provide an organization for everyone in the plumbing trades. The UA has almost four hundred thousand members in the United States, Canada, and Australia. It provides apprenticeship programs, journeyman training, instructor training in the plumbing industry, and certifications. It also has a department of political and legislative affairs, which lobbies for pro-labor policies and political candidates, as well as issues that might affect its members.

In addition to the UA labor union, there is also the Plumbing-Heating-Cooling Contractors Association (PHCCA), which works for the advancement and education of plumbers in its industry. It provides business training and education as well as attracts new workers to the industry and helps contractors use new technology to improve their performance. It also sponsors apprentice, journeyman, and business-management training, as well as holds conferences and trade shows for its members.

The American Society of Plumbing Engineers (ASPE) is an organization for professionals in the fields of plumbing system design, specifications, and inspection. It provides technical data and information; sponsors communication and networking; and through research and education, expands the base of knowledge for the plumbing industry.

Get Started!

Clearly, being a plumber isn't just about getting your hands dirty and your shoes wet as you fix a leaky pipe in someone's basement. It's a job that requires training, skill, knowledge, and a willingness to never stop learning. It's about preparing for a newer, greener world of building construction, of dealing with emergencies and adapting to new technologies that make plumbing systems more efficient. But most important, it's about providing a valuable service to the people around you,

Plumbers have training, skills, and knowledge, making them a valued part of their communities.

friends and neighbors in your city or town, when they need you the most. A plumber is an irreplaceable part of his or her community, in good times and in bad, with skills that will always be needed for the basic health and safety of people everywhere. Not many jobs can claim that.

GLOSSARY

AFFILIATE A person or organization that is officially attached to or part of a larger group.

APTITUDE A natural ability to do something.

BLUEPRINT A design plan, diagram, or other technical drawing.

COMPONENT A part or element of a larger whole, especially a part of a machine or a vehicle.

DEDUCTIVE Describes a decision or plan based on reason and the logical analysis of available facts.

DELEGATE To trust another person, who is usually not as high ranking or experienced, with a task or responsibility.

DEXTERITY Having skill in performing tasks, especially those done with the hands.

FELONY A serious crime, usually involving violence, that is punished by imprisonment.

FITTING Small detachable part for machines or systems.

HURRICANE A large tropical storm system with high circular winds.

HYDROELECTRIC Having to do with creating electricity from the flow of water.

INDUCTIVE Describes a form of reasoning based on collecting information and drawing conclusions based on observation.

MUNICIPALITY A city of town that is incorporated and has a local government.

OIL RIG A structure with equipment for drilling or servicing an oil well.

REFERRAL The act of recommending someone or something, such as a business or service, based on a positive experience with them.

SEPTIC Having to do with a household draining system that carries waste to a septic tank.

SPECIFICATION A detailed description of the design and materials used to make something and the standard of workmanship that must be met.

SUBSIDE To become less intense, violent, or severe.

SUMP A depression in the floor of a basement where water collects.

VALVE A device for controlling the flow of fluids through a pipe or duct.

FOR MORE INFORMATION

American Society of Plumbing Engineers (ASPE)
6400 Shafer Court, Suite 350
Rosemont, IL 60018-4914
(847) 296-0002
Website: https://aspe.org
ASPE is dedicated to advancing the plumbing engineering profession and protecting the public's health.

American Society of Sanitary Engineering (ASSE)
ASSE International
18927 Hickory Creek Drive, Suite 220
Mokena, IL 60448
(708) 995-3019
Website: http://www.asse-plumbing.org
ASSE works for education, public awareness, quality
control, and the reliability of plumbing systems.

American Water Works Association (AWWA)
6666 W. Quincy Avenue
Denver, CO 80235
(800) 926-7337
Website: http://www.awwa.org
A scientific and educational organization dedicated to
managing and treating water and protecting public
health and the environment.

Canadian Institute of Plumbing and Heating
295 The West Mall, Suite 504
Toronto, ON M9C 4Z4
Canada
(800) 639-247
Website: http://www.ciph.com
This association represents companies that manufacture,
sell, and distribute plumbing equipment and services.

Plumbing Heating Cooling Contractors Association
    (PHCCA)
180 S. Washington Street, Suite 100
Falls Church, VA 22046
(800) 533-7694
Web site: http://www.phccweb.org
This organization is dedicated to the advancement and
    education of the plumbing and HVAC industries.

United Association (UA) Canada
442 rue Gilmour Street
Ottawa, ON K2P 0R8
Canada
(613) 565-1100
Website: http://www.uacanada.ca
The United Association is a trade union for plumbers,
    pipe fitters, and the plumbing industry in Canada.

World Plumbing Council
Website: http://worldplumbing.org/index.html
The World Plumbing Council develops and pro-
    motes the image and standards of the plumbing
    industry all over the world.

Websites

Because of the changing nature of Internet links,
Rosen Publishing has developed an online list of
websites related to the subject of this book. This
site is updated regularly. Please use this link to
access this list:

http://www.rosenlinks.com/CIYC/Plumb

FOR FURTHER READING

Boraas, Tracey. *Community Helpers: Plumbers.* Mankato, MN: Capstone Press, 2006.

Carter, W. Hodding. *Flushed: How the Plumber Saved Civilization.* New York, NY: Atria Books, 2007.

Frankel, Michael, and R. Woodson. *Plumbers' Licensing Study Guide.* 3rd edition. New York, NY: McGraw-Hill Professional, 2012.

Frew, Katherine. *Plumber.* New York, NY: Children's Press/Scholastic, 2004.

Gregory, Josh. *Cool Careers: Plumber.* North Mankato, MN: Cherry Lake Publishing, 2011.

Joyce, Michael A. *Blueprint Reading and Drafting for Plumbers.* Farmington Hills, MI: Cengage Learning, 2008.

Joyce, Michael A., and Ray Holder. *Residential Construction Academy: Plumbing.* 2nd edition. Farmington Hills, MI: Cengage Learning, 2011.

Meister, Cari. *Community Helpers: Plumber.* Minneapolis, MN: Jump!, 2014.

National Center for Construction Education. *Plumbing Level 1 Trainee Guide.* 4th edition. Upper Saddle River, NJ: Pearson, 2012.

NCCER. *Plumbing Level 1 Trainee Guide.* 4th Edition. New York, NY: Prentice Hall, 2012.

NCCER. *Plumbing Level 2 Trainee Guide*. 4th Edition. New York, NY: Prentice Hall, 2013.

NCCER. *Plumbing Level 3 Trainee Guide.* 4th Edition. New York, NY: Prentice Hall, 2012.

Nixon, James. *What We Do: Plumber.* New York, NY: Franklin Watts, 2014.

Payment, Simone. *Essential Careers: A Career as a Plumber.* New York, NY: Rosen Publishing Group, 2010.

PHCC Educational Foundation. *Plumbing 101.* Farmington Hills, MI: Cengage Learning, 2012.

PHCC Educational Foundation. *Plumbing 201.* Farmington Hills, MI: Cengage Learning, 2008.

PHCC Educational Foundation. *Plumbing 301.* Farmington Hills, MI: Cengage Learning, 2001.

PHCC Educational Foundation. *Plumbing 401.* Farmington Hills, MI: Cengage Learning, 2008.

Ripka, L.V. *Plumbing Design and Installation.* Orlando Park, IL: American Technical Publishers, 2011.

Smith, Lee. *Mathematics for Plumbers and Pipefitters.* Farmington Hills, MI: Cengage, 2012.

BIBLIOGRAPHY

All Area Plumbing, LLC. "Two Days in the life of a Plumber." April 4, 2014. Retrieved September 21, 2014 (http://blog.allareaplumbing.net/blog/two-days -in-the-life-of-a-plumber).

American Society of Plumbing Engineers. "About ASPE." 2012. Retrieved October 11, 2014 (https:// aspe.org/about).

ApprenticeServices.com. "A Day in the Life of an Apprentice Plumber." October 18, 2011. Retrieved September 16, 2014 (http://apprenticeservices.com .au/apprenticeships/apprentice-plumber).

Art Plumbing and Air Conditioning. "A Day in the Life of a Plumber." Retrieved September 16, 2014 (http:// www.artplumbingandac.com/coral-springs-plumber/ plumbing/coral-springs-plumber).

CareerOverview.com. "Plumbing Careers, Jobs and Training Information." 2014. Retrieved September 22, 2014 (http://www.careeroverview.com/plumbing -careers.html).

Carrns, Ann. "For plumbers, It's All About the Sweet Smell of Money." Marketplace.org, March 25, 2014. Retrieved September 15, 2014 (http://www .marketplace.org/topics/your-money/work-america/ plumbers-it%E2%80%99s-all-about-sweet-smell -money).

CNN Library. "Hurricane Sandy Fast Facts." Retrieved September 15, 2014 (http://www.cnn.com/2013/ 07/13/world/americas/hurricane-sandy-fast-facts).

Education Portal. "How to Become a Plumber: Educa- tion and Career Roadmap." Retrieved September 21, 2014 (http://education-portal.com/how_to _become_a_plumber.html).

Education Portal. "Master Plumber: Education Require- ments and Career Overview." Retrieved September

21, 2014 (http://education-portal.com/articles/
Master_Plumber_Education_Requirements_and
_Career_Overview.html).

E-Plumbing Courses.com. "A Day in the Life of a Commercial Plumber." Retrieved September 16, 2014
(http://www.eplumbingcourses.com/day-in-the-life
-of-a-commercial-plumber).

Federal Emergency Management Agency. "Building
Codes." Retrieved September 22, 2014 (http://www
.fema.gov/earthquake/building-codes).

Graham, Ruth. "What It's Like to Be a Female Pipefitter."
The Grindstone, April 30, 2012. Retrieved September
16, 2014 (http://www.thegrindstone.com/2012/
04/30/mentors/what-its-like-to-be-a-female
-pipefitter-461).

Keefe Tech. "Plumbing." Retrieved September 15, 2014
(http://www.keefetech.org/page2/page42/index.html).

Marine Insight.com. "Different Jobs in a Shipyard &
Shipbuilding Industry." April 8, 2011. Retrieved September 22, 2014 (http://www.marineinsight.com/
careers-2/shore/different-jobs-in-a-shipyard
-shipbuilding-industry).

Martindale, Scott, and Elysse James. "O.C. High
Schools Boost Focus on Career Training." Orange
County Register, March 15, 2013. Retrieved September 21, 2014 (http://www.ocregister.com/news/
high-499917-school-career.html).

Montana Department of Labor and Industry. "Registered Apprenticeship & Training Program." Retrieved
September 16, 2014 (http://wsd.dli.mt.gov/
apprenticeship/atpstudents.asp).

MyJobSearch.com. "Plumber." Retrieved September
15, 2014 (http://www.myjobsearch.com/careers/
plumber.html).

New Hampshire Department of Education. "Plumbing Curriculum, 2013–2014." Retrieved September 22, 2014 (http://www.education.nh.gov/career/career/plumb_curriculum.htm).

O*Net OnLine. "Bright Outlook Occupation: 47-2152.02 – Plumbers." Retrieved October 11, 2014 (http://www.onetonline.org/help/bright/47-2152.02).

O*Net OnLine. "Summary report 47-2152.02 for Plumbers." Retrieved September 21, 2014 (http://www.onetonline.org/link/summary/47-2152.02).

PlumberTests.com. "Journeyman Plumber Exam and Licensure." 2010. Retrieved September 21, 2014 (http://www.plumbertests.com/journeyman-exam).

PlumberTests.com. "Master Plumber Exam and Licensure." 2010. Retrieved September 21, 2014 (http://www.plumbertests.com/master-exam).

Plumbing-Heating-Cooling Contractors Association. "Home Page." Retrieved October 12, 2014 (http://www.phccweb.org).

Rush, Morgan. "How to Open a Plumbing Business." Chron.com, 2014. Accessed September 21, 2014 (http://smallbusiness.chron.com/open-plumbing-business-2467.html).

Springfield Housing Authority. "A Plumbing Apprenticeship Includes Hands-On Learning and Friendship." Retrieved September 22, 2014 (http://shamass.org/2014/05/plumbing-apprenticeship-includes-hands-learning-friendship).

U.S. Army. "Careers & Jobs: Plumber." Retrieved September 22, 2014 (http://www.goarmy.com/careers-and-jobs/browse-career-and-job-categories/construction-engineering/plumber.html).

U.S. Department of Labor Statistics. "Occupational Outlook Handbook: Plumbers, Pipefitters, and

Steamfitters." January 8, 2014. Retrieved September 15, 2014 (http://www.bls.gov/ooh/construction -and-extraction/plumbers-pipefitters-and -steamfitters.htm).

U.S. Environmental Protection Agency. "Green Build-ing." October 9, 2014. Retrieved October 11, 2014 (http://www.epa.gov/greenbuilding/pubs/faqs.htm).

Vocations.com. "Plumber vs Electrician vs HVAC Tech—What's the Difference?" Retrieved September 16, 2014 (http://www.trade-certificates.com/trades/ plumber-electrician-hvac-tech-whats-the-difference).

Washington State Department of Labor & Industries. "Plumber Exams." Retrieved September 21, 2014 (http://www.lni.wa.gov/TradesLicensing/Plumbing/ TestCert/Exams).

World Plumbing Day.org. "World Plumbing Day Makes a Splash!" 2012. Retrieved September 21, 2014 (http:// www.worldplumbingday.org/~world316/index.php ?option=com_content&view=article&catid=4:news &id=35:world-plumbing-day-makes-a-splash).

Yadav, Monica. "The Importance of Plumbers on National Plumbers Day." Direct Energy, April 23, 2014. Retrieved October 11, 2014 (http://www .directenergy.com/newsroom/press-releases/ 2014/the-importance-of-national-plumbers-day).

INDEX

About the Author

Marcia Amidon Lusted is the author of 100 books and more than 450 magazine articles for young readers. She is also an editor for Cricket Media, developing children's books, magazines, and digital products. She works with vo-tech program at her local high school and sees firsthand students who begin pursuing careers like plumbing before they have even graduated. She lives in New Hampshire. Visit her at www.adventuresinnonfiction.com.

Photo Credits

Cover © iStockphoto.com/MachineHeadz; pp. 5, 14 Robert Nickelsberg/Getty Images; p. 9 © iStockphoto.com/Spiderstock; pp. 10–11 Henrik Sorensen/Stone/Getty Images; p. 16 Chris Sattlberger/Photographer's Choice/Getty Images; p. 18 Alex Raths/iStock/Thinkstock; pp. 21, 67 Paul Bradbury/Caiaimage/Getty Images; p. 24 sturti/Vetta/Getty Images; p. 26 Monkey Business Images/Shutterstock.com; p. 27 Echo/Cultura/Getty Images; p. 31 Jupiterimages/Photolibrary/Getty Images; p. 34 monkeybusinessimages/iStock/Thinkstock; p. 37 Jon Feingersh/Blend Images/Getty Images; p. 39 Arthur Carlo Franco/Vetta/Getty Images; p. 41 © AP Images; p. 43 © Studioshots/Alamy; p. 48 Bart Coenders/E+/Getty Images; p. 51 © Alistair Laming/Alamy; p. 52 © Richard Sennott/Minneapolis Star Tribune/ZUMA Press; p. 54 © Cultura Creative (RF)/Alamy; p. 56 Thaier Al-Sudani/Reuters/Newscom; p. 61 JackF/iStock/Thinkstock; p. 63 Spencer Platt/Getty Images; p. 64 Roy Mehta/Photographer's Choice/Getty Images; cover and interior pages border and background images © iStockphoto.com/polygraphus (pipes), © iStockphoto.com/Pingebat (map).

Designer: Nicole Russo; Editor: Christine Poolos